Oregon
Facts and Symbols

by Emily McAuliffe

Consultant:
Adair Law
Director of Publications
Oregon Historical Society

Capstone *press*

Mankato, Minnesota

Capstone Press
151 Good Counsel Drive, P.O. Box 669, Mankato, Minnesota 56002
http://www.capstone-press.com

Library of Congress Cataloging-in-Publication Data
McAuliffe, Emily
   Oregon facts and symbols/by Emily McAuliffe.—Rev. and updated ed.
   p. cm.—(The states and their symbols)
   Includes bibliographical references (p. 23) and index.
   Summary: Presents information about the state of Oregon, its nickname, motto, and emblems.
   ISBN 0-7368-2267-4 (hardcover)
   1. Emblems, State—Oregon—Juvenile literature. I. Title. II. Series: McAuliffe, Emily. States and their symbols.
CR203.07M38 2003
979.5—dc21   2002154839

Editorial Credits
Christianne C. Jones, update editor; Chuck Miller, editor; Linda Clavel, update designer and illustrator; Steve Christensen, cover designer; Wanda Winch, update photo researcher; Kimberly Danger, photo researcher

Photo Credits
Corbis/Kennan Ward, cover
John Elk III, 10, 22 (middle)
Jon Gnass/Jon Gnass Photo Images, 6
Mark Turner, 16
Maxine Cass, 22 (top)
One Mile Up, Inc., 8, 10 (inset)
Oregon Coast Aquarium, 22 (bottom)
Robert McCaw, 18
Sally Weigand, 14
Visuals Unlimited/Barbara Cerlach, 12; Glenn M. Oliver, 20

Table of Contents

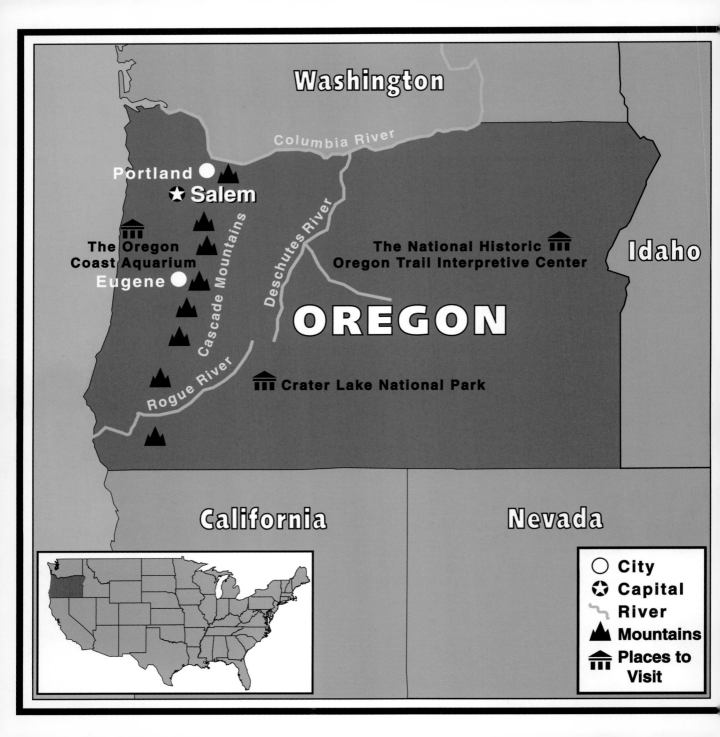

Fast Facts

Capital: Salem is the capital of Oregon.

Largest City: Portland is the largest city in Oregon. Almost 530,000 people live in Portland.

Size: Oregon covers 98,386 square miles (254,820 square kilometers). It is the 9th largest state.

Location: Oregon is located in the northwestern United States.

Population: 3,421,399 people live in Oregon (2000 U.S. Census Bureau).

Statehood: Oregon became the 33rd state on February 14, 1859.

Natural Resources: Lumber, stone, and fish are all important natural resources in Oregon.

Manufactured Goods: Oregon's businesses produce wood, paper, electronics, and paper products.

Crops: Oregon farmers grow sugar beets, berries, wheat, and hazelnuts. Farmers in eastern Oregon also raise cattle.

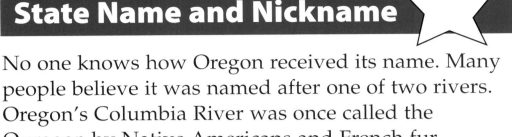

State Name and Nickname

No one knows how Oregon received its name. Many people believe it was named after one of two rivers. Oregon's Columbia River was once called the Ouragan by Native Americans and French fur traders. Ouragan is a French word that means storm. The Columbia River is powerful like a storm.

Others say Oregon's name comes from an early French fur trader's map. Oregon's Wisconsin River was named Ouaricon-sint on the map.

Oregon's state nickname is the Beaver State. This nickname reminds Oregonians of the state's early fur traders. The fur traders trapped thousands of beavers during the 1800s. Hatmakers in Europe bought the thick, soft beaver fur to make hats.

Settlers also admired beavers. The settlers saw that beavers worked hard cutting down trees and building their homes. The beavers' hard work reminded settlers of their own work habits.

Some people believe Oregon might be named after the Columbia River.

State Seal and Motto

Oregon adopted its state seal in 1903. The state seal reminds Oregonians of their state's government. The seal placed on papers makes them official.

Oregon's seal shows a shield surrounded by 33 stars. Oregon was the 33rd state to join the United States. Forests, mountains, and oceans appear on the shield. They stand for Oregon's natural environment. The seal also displays a British navy ship leaving Oregon. A North American merchant ship sails toward the state. The ships stand for Oregon becoming a U.S. territory.

Oregon has had two state mottos. The motto "Union" was adopted in 1957. This motto honored the United States. The motto changed in 1987. Oregon's motto is now "She flies with her own wings." This motto means Oregonians like their state to be independent.

An ox team pulling a covered wagon appears on the seal. The image reminds Oregonians of early settlers.

STATE OF OREGON

THE UNION

1859

Salem is the capital of Oregon. Oregon's state government meets in the capital city.

The capitol building stands in Salem. It is Oregon's third capitol building. Oregon's first two capitols were built of wood. Fires destroyed these buildings in 1871 and 1935.

Workers finished building the current capitol in 1938. It is made of white marble from Vermont. A tower rises from the top of the capitol. A gold statue called the Oregon Pioneer sits on top of the tower. The statue faces west in honor of Oregon's early settlers. They traveled west to reach the state.

Oregon's state flag was adopted in 1925. The flag is dark blue and gold. The state seal appears on one side of the flag. The other side shows Oregon's state animal, the American beaver. Oregon has the only state flag with a design on both sides.

The Oregon Pioneer faces west in honor of Oregon's early settlers. The statue is 23 feet (7 meters) tall.

State Bird

The western meadowlark became Oregon's state bird in 1927. The meadowlark lives in the central and western United States. Meadowlarks live on plains and in meadows. The bird is 8 to 11 inches (20 to 28 centimeters) long.

The meadowlark is a colorful bird. It has a bright yellow chest. The meadowlark also has a black ring of feathers around its neck.

The meadowlark is known for its beautiful song. The bird can sing as many as 200 notes per minute. Males sing more often than females.

Meadowlarks build nests covered with grass and weeds. Female meadowlarks lay 3 to 7 eggs in their nests. The eggs are white with purple or brown spots.

Meadowlark eggs hatch in about two weeks. Adult meadowlarks gather insects and grain to feed their young. The young eat and grow. They leave the nest about two weeks after hatching.

Meadowlarks have bright yellow chests. Male meadowlarks have brighter feathers than females.

State Tree

The Douglas fir became Oregon's state tree in 1939. Douglas firs grow along Oregon's Pacific coast.

Douglas firs are one of the tallest types of trees in the world. They can grow to be 200 feet (61 meters) tall. Their trunks can sometimes measure as much as 6 feet (1.8 meters).

The wood from a Douglas fir is strong but light. This feature makes it one of the best trees to use for lumber. The lumber industry is one of Oregon's most important businesses. Workers cut down Douglas firs to make lumber.

Parts of Oregon's forests are protected by the government. No one can cut down Douglas firs in these areas. Lumber companies must plant trees after clearing areas of forest that are not protected.

Douglas firs are evergreen trees. They stay green all year.

State Flower

Oregon's state flower is the Oregon grape plant. Government officials made it the state flower in 1899.

Oregon grape plants grow along the state's Pacific coast. The plants rarely grow east of Oregon's Cascade Mountains.

Tiny yellow flowers bloom on the Oregon grape plant in early summer. The flowers become dark blue berries in the fall. These berries are sweeter than grapes that grow in other parts of the United States. Cooks sometimes use the berries to make desserts.

People also use the Oregon grape plant to make medicine. They cut off the roots of the plants and dry them. The roots can help relieve some skin and stomach illnesses.

Oregon grape plants grow close to the ground. They are evergreen plants. Shiny green leaves cover their branches all year.

Oregon grape plant blossoms are bright yellow. The flowers become dark blue berries in the fall.

State Animal

The American beaver became Oregon's state animal in 1969. Beavers are large, brown rodents. Beavers and other rodents have long front teeth.

Adult beavers weigh 35 to 65 pounds (16 to 29 kilograms). Beavers have black tails that are large and flat. Their tails help beavers swim. Beavers also use their tails to alert other beavers of danger. They slap their tails on water before diving to safety.

Beavers have strong front teeth. Beavers gnaw on trees to keep their teeth from growing too long.

Beavers live in lodges that they build from small trees and bushes. Beavers cut down trees with their teeth. They then pile up the branches to build dome-shaped lodges.

Fur traders once caught too many beavers in Oregon and the United States. The animals almost disappeared. Today, the number of beavers is growing throughout the United States.

Beavers use branches from small trees and bushes to build their lodges.

State Dance: In 1977, officials chose the square dance as Oregon's state dance. Western pioneers invented this dance. Oregon's officials thought it represented a part of the state's history.

State Fish: The Chinook salmon became Oregon's state fish in 1961. Chinook salmon can grow to be 5 feet (1.5 meters) long. Many people in Oregon like fishing for Chinook salmon.

State Gemstone: In 1987, the sunstone became Oregon's state gemstone. Sunstones are brightly colored stones. Light can shine through them.

State Nut: Officials chose the hazelnut as the state nut in 1989. Oregon grows almost all of the hazelnuts in the United States.

State Song: Oregon's state song is "Oregon, My Oregon." It was written by J.A. Buchanan and Henry B. Murtahg.

Many Oregonians like fishing for Chinook salmon. This fish is the largest member of the Pacific salmon family.

Places to Visit

Crater Lake

Crater Lake is in Klamath County. Lava from a nearby volcano formed a huge crater there 6,800 years ago. Rain and snow filled the crater after the lava cooled. Crater Lake is the deepest lake in the United States. Visitors hike around the lake. They also fish or boat on this lake.

National Historic Oregon Trail Interpretive Center

Between 1840 and 1870, more than 250,000 settlers headed west to Oregon. They traveled in covered wagons along the Oregon Trail. The National Historic Oregon Trail Interpretive Center is near Baker City. Visitors learn about pioneer life. They also see wheel ruts left by settlers' wagons.

Oregon Coast Aquarium

The Oregon Coast Aquarium is on Yaquina Bay in Newport. The aquarium is home to more than 8,000 animals. Visitors come face to face with sea otters, seals, and sharks. Several exhibits display animals and plant life from Oregon's coastline.

Words to Know

evergreen (EV-ur-green)—a tree that stays green all year
gnaw (NAW)—to bite or chew; beavers gnaw on branches.
lodge (LOJ)—a beaver's home; beavers use branches and mud to build lodges in lakes and rivers.
lumber (LUHM-bur)—wood from a tree; lumber is cut from trees after they are sawed down.
medicine (MED-uh-suhn)—a drug or other material used to treat someone who is sick; the root of the Oregon grape plant can be used as medicine.
pioneer (pye-uh-NEER)—someone who explores an unknown land and settles there; many European pioneers began moving to Oregon in the 1840s.
rodent (ROHD-uhnt)—a small mammal with long front teeth used for gnawing; a beaver is a rodent.

Read More

Capstone Press Geography Department. *Oregon.* One Nation. Mankato, Minn.: Capstone Press, 2003.
Bratvold, Gretchen. *Oregon.* Hello U.S.A. Minneapolis: Lerner Publications, 2003.
Heinrichs, Ann. *Oregon.* The Land is your Land. Minneapolis: Compass Point Books, 2003.

Useful Addresses

Oregon History Center
1200 Southwest Park Blvd.
Portland, OR 97201

Oregon Secretary of State
Information Systems Division
Public Service Building
Suite 103
Salem, OR 97310

Internet Sites

Do you want to find out more about Oregon?
Let FactHound, our fact-finding hound dog, do the
research for you.

Here's how:
1) Visit **http://www.facthound.com**
2) Type in the **BOOK ID** number:
   0736822674
3) Click on **FETCH IT**.

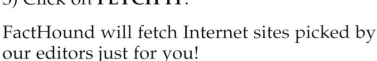

FactHound will fetch Internet sites picked by
our editors just for you!

Index